How to be Filled with the Holy Spirit

How to be Filled with the Holy Spirit

by

A. W. Tozer

MOCKINGBIRD
PRESS

Copyright © 2022 Mockingbird Press

All rights reserved. The original works are in the public domain to the best of publisher's knowledge. The publisher makes no claim to the original writings. However, the compilation, construction, cover design, trademarks, derivations, foreword, descriptions, added work, etc., of this edition are copyrighted and may not be reproduced, distributed, or transmitted in any form or by any means, including photocopying, recording, or other electronic or mechanical methods, without the prior written permission of the publisher, except in the case of brief quotations embodied in critical reviews and certain other non-commercial uses permitted by copyright law, or where content is specifically noted as being reproduced under a Creative Commons license.

Cover, "Landschaft," by Christian Rohlfs, 1903
Foreword, Copyright © 2022 Mockingbird Press, LLC
Cover Design by Matthew Johnson, Copyright © 2022 Mockingbird Press LLC
Interior Design by Daria Lacy

Publisher's Cataloging-In-Publication Data

Tozer, A.W., author; with Underhill, Rachael, Forward by
How to by Filled with the Holy Spirit / A.W. Tozer; with Rachael Underhill.

Paperback	ISBN-13: 978-1-68493-012-8
Hardback	ISBN-13: 978-1-68493-013-5
Ebook	ISBN-13: 978-1-68493-014-2

1. Religion—Christian Living—General. 2. Philosophy & Religion—Religion & Beliefs—Christianity—Christian Life & Practice, I. A.W. Tozer. II. Rachael Underhill. III. How to be Filled with the Holy Spirit.

REL012000 / QRMP

Type Set in Century Schoolbook / **Franklin Gothic Demi**

Mockingbird Press, Augusta, GA
info@mockingbirdpress.com

CONTENTS

Foreword vii
Preface 1
Who is the Holy Spirit? 3
The Promise of the Father 13
How to be Filled, with the Holy Spirit 23
How to Cultivate the Spirit's Companionship 33

Foreword

How to Be Filled with the Holy Spirit, first published in 1952, is a collection of four sermons by preacher and writer A.W. Tozer. The series explains the Christian relationship to the Holy Spirit—who He is, and how to receive Him.

A.W. Tozer (1897-1963) was a self-educated pastor, writer, and mentor. He spent his career preaching and educating with the Christian and Missionary Alliance. He wrote for the group's magazine *Alliance Weekly*, as well as for other publications like *Christian Life*.

During his life he wrote 12 books on Christianity, in addition to dozens of essays and sermons. Many of his shorter writings have been collected into books like this one, sharing the great man's thoughts on specific themes.

Tozer's fundamentalism was built on a foundation of prayer, which he advocated to his congregants. He prayed for several hours each day, building his personal relationship with God.

How to Be Filled with the Holy Spirit provides a deep exploration of the third—and least understood—part of the Holy Trinity.

The first sermon, titled *Who is the Holy Spirit*, begins with an explanation of who exactly He is. For He is a Person, although one that is not made of physical matter. "He is a Person..." Tozer writes, "with all the qualities and powers of personality. He is not matter, but He is substance."

As a spirit, He can penetrate physical matter. He can be all around us and within us, if we are ready to receive Him. Tozer writes, "He has not weight, nor measure, nor size, nor any color, no extension in space, but He nevertheless exists as surely as you exist."

But who is He exactly? Using proof from scripture, creeds, and hymns, he shows that the Holy Spirit is no more and no less than God the Creator Himself. Placed on equal footing with the Father and the Son in scripture, the third corner of that triangle must be equally divine.

In the second sermon, *The Promise of the Father*, Tozer explains how the Holy Spirit came to us here on Earth. The arrival of the Holy Spirit is the realization of God the Father's promise to us. The Holy Spirit is God's gift, sent back after Christ's resurrection and ascension.

Upon His arrival, He filled the followers of Jesus Christ. And He is still here, ready to fill those of us who are prepared and ask to be filled.

The next sermon, *How to be Filled with the Holy Spirit*, asks vital questions. Are you sure you want to be filled with the Spirit? Tozer asks, "Do you want Him to be Lord of your life? That you want His benefits, I know ... But do you want to be possessed by Him? ... Are you sure that you want your personality to be taken over by One who will expect obedience to the written and living Word?"

After all, to be filled with the Holy Spirit means you must live your life in and for Christ. You must reject the worldliness in which you have been raised. You may not tolerate evil, turning a blind eye to anything that would displease God. To get closer to God, you must get further away from the world.

But for those that would be filled, Tozer explains the necessary steps. Simple, but not easy.

The final sermon explains *How to Cultivate the Spirit's Companionship*. For those who are fully committed, they must treat the Holy Spirit as a living Person and honor the Lord Jesus Christ. "As we honor Jesus," he says, "the Spirit of God becomes glad within us. He ceases to hold back, He relaxes and becomes intimate and communes and imparts Himself; and the sun comes up and heaven comes near as Jesus Christ becomes our all in all."

In the preface to this collection, Tozer apologizes for the "racy style" in these sermons, stating that "Had [he] been writing the messages, [he] would have taken greater care in the composition." But in fact, it is this casual style that makes the sermons so effective. The reader can imagine sitting with a trusted spiritual mentor, receiving life-changing personal advice from someone who has themselves been filled with the Holy Spirit.

Preface

The following pages represent the gist of a series of sermons given on successive Sunday evenings to the congregation of the church of which I am pastor. The talks were taken down stenographically and later reduced to their present length. A fifth message which was a part of the series has been omitted here.

The fact that these were originally spoken messages accounts for their racy style and for the personal references which occur in them occasionally. Had I been writing the messages I should have exercised greater care in the composition. The subject is, however, so vitally important that I feel sure the reader will pardon the offhand style of the language. The truth is always good even when the vehicle in which it rides is homely and plain.

This booklet is made available to the Christian public with the prayer that it may help to lead many thirsty believers to the fountain of living waters.

—A. W. T.

Who is the Holy Spirit?

We all use the word "spirit" a great deal. Now I want to tell you what I do and do not mean by it. In the first place, we rule out all of the secondary uses of the word "spirit." I do not mean courage, as when we say, "That's the spirit!" I don't mean temper or temperament or pluck. I mean nothing so nebulous as that. Spirit is a specific and identifiable substance. If not definable, it can at least be described. Spirit is as real as matter, but it is another mode of being than matter.

We are all materialists to some extent. We are born of material parents into a material world; we are wrapped in material clothes and fed on material milk and lie in a material bed, and sleep and walk and live and talk and grow up in a world of matter. Matter presses upon us obtrusively and takes over our thinking so completely that we cannot speak of spirit without using materialistic terms. God made man out of the dust of the ground, and man has been dust ever since, and we can't quite shake it off.

Matter is one mode of being; spirit is another mode of being as authentic as matter.

Material things have certain characteristics. For instance, they have weight. Everything that is material weighs something; it yields to gravitational pull. Then, matter has dimensions; you can measure the thing if it is made of matter. It has shape. It has an outline of some sort, no matter whether it is a molecule or an atom or whatever it may be, on up to the stars that shine. Then, it is extended in space. So I say that weight, dimension, shape and extension are the things that belong to matter. That is one mode of being; that is one way of existing.

One power of spirit, of any spirit (for I am talking about spirit now, not about the Holy Spirit), is its ability to penetrate. Matter bumps against other matter and stops; it cannot penetrate. Spirit can penetrate everything. For instance, your body is made of matter, and yet your spirit has penetrated your body completely. Spirit can penetrate spirit. It can penetrate personality—oh, if God's people could only learn that spirit can penetrate personality, that your personality is not an impenetrable substance, but can be penetrated. A mind can be penetrated by thought, and the air can be penetrated by light, and material things and mental things, and even spiritual things, can be penetrated by spirit.

Now, what is the Holy Spirit? Not who, but what? The answer is that the Holy Spirit is a Being dwelling in another mode of existence. He has not weight, nor measure, nor size, nor any color, no extension in space, but He nevertheless exists as surely as you exist.

The Holy Spirit is not enthusiasm. I have found enthusiasm that hummed with excitement, and the Holy

Spirit was nowhere to be found there at all; and I have found the Holy Ghost when there has not been much of what we call enthusiasm present. Neither is the Holy Spirit another name for genius. We talk about the spirit of Beethoven and say, "This or that artist played with great spirit. He interpreted the spirit of the master." The Holy Spirit is none of these things. Now what is He?

He is a Person. Put that down in capital letters—that the Holy Spirit is not only a Being having another mode of existence, but He is Himself a Person, with all the qualities and powers of personality. He is not matter, but He is substance. The Holy Spirit is often thought of as a beneficent wind that blows across the Church. If you think of the Holy Spirit as being literally a wind, a breath, then you think of Him as nonpersonal and nonindividual. But the Holy Spirit has will and intelligence and feeling and knowledge and sympathy and ability to love and see and flunk and hear and speak and desire the same as any person has.

You may say, "I believe all that. You surely don't think you are telling us anything new!" I don't hope to tell you very much that is new; I only hope to set the table for you, arranging the dishes a little better and a little more attractively so that you will be tempted to partake. Many of us have grown up on the theology that accepts the Holy Spirit as a Person, and even as a divine Person, but for some reason it never did us any good. We are as empty as ever, we are as joyless as ever, we are as far from peace as ever, we are as weak as ever. What I want to do is to tell you the old things, but while I am doing it, to encourage your heart to make them yours now, and to walk into the living, throbbing, vibrating heart of them, so that from here on your life will be altogether different.

So the Spirit is a Person. That's what He is. Now, who is He?

The historic church has said that He is God. Let me quote from the Nicene Creed: "I believe in the Holy Ghost, the Lord and Giver of life, Which proceedeth from the Father and the Son, and with the Father and the Son together is worshipped and glorified."

That is what the Church believed about the Holy Ghost 1,600 years ago. Let's be daring for a moment. Let's try to think away this idea that the Holy Spirit is truly God. All right. Let's admit something else into the picture. Let's say, "I believe in one Holy Ghost, the Lord and Giver of life, who with the Father and the Son is to be worshiped and glorified." For the "Holy Ghost" let's put in "Abraham, the father of the faithful, who with the Father and the Son together is worshiped and glorified." That is a monstrous thing, and in your heart already there is a shocked feeling. You couldn't do it. You couldn't admit a mere man into the holy circle of the Trinity! The Father and the Son are to be worshiped and glorified, and if the Holy Spirit is to be included here. He has to be equal to the Father and the Son.

Now let's look at the Athanasian Creed. Thirteen hundred years old it is. Notice what it says about the Holy Spirit: "Such as the Father is, such is the Son, and such is the Holy Ghost." Once more let's do that terrible thing. Let's introduce into this concept the name of a man. Let's put David in there. Let's say, "Such as the Father is, such also is the Son, and such is the hymnist David." That would be a shock like cold water in the face! You can't do that. And you can't put the archangel Michael in there. You can't say, "Such as the Father is, such also is the Son, and such is the archangel Michael." That would be a monstrous inconsistency, and you know it!

I have told you what the great creeds of the church say. If the Bible taught otherwise, I would throw the creeds away. Nobody can come down the years with flowing beard, and with the dust of centuries upon him, and get me to believe a doctrine unless he can give me chapter and verse. I quote the creeds, but I preach them only so far as they summarize the teaching of the Bible on a given subject. If there were divergency from the teachings of the Word of God I would not teach the creed; I would teach the Book, for the Book is the source of all authentic information. However, our fathers did a mighty good job of going into the Bible, finding out what it taught, and then formulating the creeds for us.

Now let's look at what our song writers and our hymnists believed. Recall the words the quartet sang this evening:

> *"Holy Ghost, with light divine,*
> *Shine upon this heart of mine."*

Let's pray that prayer to Gabriel, to Saint Bernard, to D. L. Moody. Let's pray that prayer to any man or any creature that has ever served God. You can't pray that kind of prayer to a creature. To put those words into a hymn means that the one about whom you are speaking must be God.

> *"Holy Ghost, with power divine,*
> *Cleanse this guilty heart of mine."*

Who can get into the intricate depths of a human soul, into the deep confines of a human spirit and cleanse it? Nobody but the God who made it! The hymn writer who said "Cleanse this guilty heart of mine" meant that the Holy Ghost to whom he prayed was God.

> *"Holy Spirit, all divine,*
> *Dwell within this heart of mine;*
> *Cast down every idol throne,*
> *Reign supreme—and reign alone."*

The church has sung that now for about one hundred years. "Reign supreme—and reign alone." Could you pray that to anybody you know? The man who wrote that hymn believed that the Holy Ghost was God, otherwise he wouldn't have said, "Reign supreme, and reign all by Yourself." That is an invitation no man can make to anybody, except the Divine One, except God.

Now the Scriptures. Notice that I am trying to establish the truth that the Holy Spirit is not only a Person, but that He is a divine Person; not only a divine Person, but God.

In Psalm 139 the hymnist attributes omnipresence to the Holy Ghost. He says, "Whither shall I go from thy spirit? or whither shall I flee from thy presence?" and he develops throughout the 139th Psalm, in language that is as beautiful as a sunrise and as musical as the wind through the willows, the idea that the Spirit is everywhere, having the attributes of deity. He must be deity, for no creature could have the attributes of deity.

In Hebrews (9: 14) there is attributed to the Holy Ghost that which is never attributed to an archangel, or a seraphim, or a cherubim, or an angel, or an apostle, or a martyr, or a prophet, or a patriarch, or anyone that has ever been created by the hand of God. It says, "Through the eternal Spirit," and every theologian knows that eternity is an attribute of no creature which deity has ever formed. The angels are not eternal; that is, they had a beginning, and all created things had beginning. As soon as the word "eternal" is used about a being it immediately establishes the fact that he never had a beginning, is not a creature at all, but God. Therefore, when the Holy Ghost says "the eternal Spirit" about Himself He is calling Himself God.

Again, the baptismal formula in Matthew 28 says, "Baptizing them in the name of the Father, and of the Son, and of the Holy Ghost." Now try to imagine putting the name of a man in there. "Baptizing them in the name of the Father and the Son and the Apostle Paul." You couldn't think it! It is horrible to contemplate! No man can be admitted into that closed circle of deity. We baptize in the name of the Father and the Son, because the Son is equal with the Father in His Godhead, and we baptize in the name of the Holy Ghost because the Holy Ghost is also equal with the Father and the Son.

You say, "You are just a Trinitarian and we are Trinitarians already." Yes, I know it, but once again I tell you that I am trying to throw emphasis upon this teaching.

How many blessed truths have gotten snowed under. People believe them, but they are just not being taught, that is all. I think of our experience this morning. Here was a man and his wife, a very fine intelligent couple from another city. They named the church to which they belonged, and I instantly said, "That is a fine church!" "Oh, yes," they said, "but they don't teach what we came over here for." They came over because they were ill and wanted to be scripturally anointed for healing. So I got together two missionaries, two preachers, and an elder, and we anointed them and prayed for them. If you were to go to that church where they attend and say to the preacher, "Do you believe that the Lord answers prayer and heals the sick?" he would reply, "Sure, I do!" He believes it, but he doesn't teach it, and what you don't believe strongly enough to teach doesn't do you any good.

It is the same with the fullness of the Holy Ghost. Evangelical Christianity believes it, but nobody experiences it. It lies under the snow, forgotten. I am praying that God may be able to melt away the ice from this blessed truth, and let it spring up again alive, that the Church and the people who hear may get some good out of it and not merely say "I believe" while it is buried under the snow of inactivity and nonattention.

Let us recapitulate. Who is the Spirit? The Spirit is God, existing in another mode of being than ourselves. He exists as a spirit and not as matter, for He is not matter, but He is God. He is a Person. It was so believed by the whole Church of Christ down through the years. It was so sung by the hymnists back in the days of the first hymn writers. It is so taught in the Book, all through the Old Testament and the New, and I have given you only a few proof texts. I could spend the evening reading Scripture stating this same thing.

Now what follows from all this? Ah, there is an unseen Deity present, a knowing, feeling Personality, and He is indivisible from the Father and the Son, so that if you were to be suddenly transferred to heaven itself you wouldn't be any closer to God than you are now, for God is already here. Changing your geographical location would not bring you any nearer to God nor God any nearer to you, because the indivisible Trinity is present, and all that the Son is the Holy Ghost is, and all that the Father is the Holy Ghost is, and the Holy Ghost is in His Church.

What will we find Him to be like? He will be exactly like Jesus. You have read your New Testament, and you know what Jesus is like, and the Holy Spirit is exactly like Jesus, for Jesus was God and the Spirit is God, and the Father is exactly like the Son; and you can know what Jesus is like by knowing what the Father is like, and you can know what the Spirit is like by knowing what Jesus is like.

If Jesus were to come walking down this aisle there would be no stampede for the door. Nobody would scream and be frightened. We might begin to weep for sheer joy and delight that He had so honored us, but nobody would be afraid of Jesus; no mother with a little crying babe would ever have to be afraid of Jesus; no poor harlot being dragged by the hair of her head had to be afraid of Jesus—nobody! Nobody ever need to be afraid of Jesus, because He is the epitome of love, kindliness, geniality, warm attractiveness and sweetness. And that is exactly what the Holy Ghost is, for He is the Spirit of the Father and the Son. Amen.

THE PROMISE OF THE FATHER

"And, behold, I send the promise of my Father upon you: but tarry ye in the city of Jerusalem, until ye be endued with power from on high" Luke 24: 49.

I wonder if you have ever thought of the origin of the phrase Jesus used here. Why did He call it the Father's promise? He didn't say "mine." He said, "The promise of my Father." This takes us back to Joel 2: 28, 29.

"And it shall come to pass afterward, that I will pour out my spirit upon all flesh; and your sons and your daughters shall prophesy, your old men shall dream dreams, your young men shall see visions: and also upon the servants and upon the handmaids in those days will I pour out my spirit."

Now, when our Lord Jesus came He authoritatively interpreted this, and tied up His intention for His Church with the ancient promises given by the Father centuries before.

In fulfillment of all this there were three periods discernible in the New Testament: (1) The period of the promise; (2) the period of the preparation, and (3) the period of the realization-all this having to do with the promise of the Father and the intention of the Son toward His people.

The period of the promise extends from John the Baptist, roughly, to the resurrection of our Lord Jesus. The marks of it are these: that there were disciples, and they were commissioned and instructed, and they exercised their commission and the authority granted them by the Lord. They knew the Lord Jesus; they loved Him. They knew Him living, they knew Him and saw Him dead, and they saw Him risen again from the dead. All the time our Lord was with them He was busy creating expectation in them. He was telling His disciples that in spite of all they had and all the blessing that God the Father had given them, they were still to expect the coming of a new and superior kind of life. He was creating an expectation of an effusion of outpoured energy which they, at their best, did not yet enjoy.

Then our Lord rose from the dead and we have what we call the period of the preparation. That was the short period which intervened between our Lord's resurrection and the down coming of the Holy Ghost. They had stopped their activity at the specific command of the Lord. He said, "Tarry! You are about to receive that which has been promised. Your expectations are about to be fulfilled; your hopes realized. Therefore, don't do anything until it comes."

I might say here that sometimes you are going farther when you are not going anywhere; you are moving faster when you are not moving at all; you are learning more when you think you have stopped learning. These disciples had reached an impasse. Their Lord had risen, and they had seen Him, and with excitement and joy they knew He had risen from the dead. Now He had gone from them. Where was He? They gathered together, as you and I might have done under like circumstances, waiting, all of one accord. That is more than they had done during the period of the promise. But here were 120 of them, and they had a oneness of accord.

The period of realization came upon them when the Father fulfilled His promise and sent the Spirit. Peter used a phrase to describe it which is one of the fullest, finest phrases I know. He said, "He hath shed forth this, which ye now see and hear"— the shedding forth was like a mighty down coming of water. The expectations were more than met—not fully met, but more than met. God always gives us an overplus. They got more than they expected.

Now what happened here? What did they receive that they had not had before? Well, first, they had a new kind of evidence for the reality of their faith. You see, Christ talked about four lines of evidence of His Messiahship.

He said: "Search the scriptures; for in them ye think ye have eternal life: and they are they which testify of me." The Scriptures were proof of who Christ was. That is one line of evidence.

Another line is the witness of John the Baptist who pointed to Jesus and said, "Behold, the Lamb of God, that taketh away the sin of the world!"

Jesus gives us another line of evidence. He said, "The Father himself . . . hath borne witness of me," and there was the third proof of His Messiahship, an authentic proof of it.

He gave a fourth. He said, "The same works that I do, bear witness of me, that the Father hath sent me." "Believe me for the very works' sake." Have you noticed there is one serious breakdown there, a breakdown which our Lord recognized and which He remedied when the Holy Spirit came? That breakdown lies in the necessary externality of the proof. In every instance the proofs which our Lord adduced to His own Messiahship were external to the individual. They are not inside of the man. He has to open the Book and read. That is external to the man.

When I hear that the Church of Christ has gone throughout the whole world carrying the torch of civilization, healing and giving hope and help, I conclude the Christian Church must be of God because she is acting the way God would act. When I hear that she has founded hospitals and insane asylums, I say surely she must be of God because that is what God would do, being what He is. When I hear that she has emancipated woman and has taken her from being a chattel slave and an object of some old king's lust to being the equal of the man and queen in his home, I say surely that must be of God. You can go down the corridors of history, and you can adduce proof of the divinity of the Church from what the Church has done. You can show how she brought civilization here and she brought help there. She cleaned up saloons in this town, and she delivered this young fellow from drink. We say that must be God. But that is external proof and it depends upon logic.

There is another kind of evidence. It is the immediate evidence of the inner life. That is the evidence by which you know you are alive. If I were to prove that you weren't alive, you would chuckle and go home just as alive as you are now and not a bit worried about it, because you have the instant, unmediated evidence of internal life.

Jesus Christ wanted to take religion out of the external and make it internal and put it on the same level as life itself, so that a man knows he knows God the same as he knows he is himself and not somebody else. He knows he knows God the same as he knows he is alive and not dead. Only the Holy Ghost can do that. The Holy Spirit came to carry the evidence of Christianity from the books of apologetics into the human heart, and that is exactly what He does. You can take the gospel of Jesus Christ to the heathen in Borneo, or Africa, people who could never conceive the first premise of your logical arguments, so that it would be totally impossible for them to decide on logical grounds whether Christianity was of God or not. Preach Christ to them and they will believe and be transformed and put away their wickedness and change from evil to righteousness and get happy about it all, learn to read and write and study their Bibles and become leaders and pillars in their church, transformed and made over. How? By the instant witness of the Holy Ghost to their hearts. This is the new thing that came, sir! God took religion from the realm of the external and made it internal.

Our trouble is that we are trying to confirm the truth of Christianity by an appeal to external evidence. We are saying, "Well, look at this fellow. He can throw a baseball farther than anybody else and he is a Christian, therefore Christianity must be true." "Here is a great statesman who believes the Bible. Therefore, the Bible must be true." We quote Daniel Webster, or Roger Bacon. We write books to show that some scientist believed in Christianity: therefore, Christianity must be true. We are all the way out on the wrong track, brother! That is not New Testament Christianity at all. That is a pitiful, whimpering, drooling appeal to the flesh. That never was the testimony of the New Testament, never the way God did things—never! You might satisfy the intellects of men by external evidences, and Christ did, I say, point to external evidence when He was here on the earth. But He said, "I am sending you something better. I am taking Christian apologetics out of the realm of logic and putting it into the realm of life. I am proving My deity, and My proof will not be an appeal to a general or a prime minister. The proof lies in an invisible, unseen but powerful energy that visits the human soul when the gospel is preached—the Holy Ghost!" The Spirit of the living God brought an evidence that needed no logic; it went straight to the soul like a flash of silver light, like the direct plunge of a sharp spear into the heart. Those are the very words that the Scriptures use when it says "pierced (pricked) to the heart." One translator points out that that word "pricked" is a word that means that it goes in deeper than the spear that pierced Jesus' side!

That is the way God does. There is an immediate witness, an unmediated push of the Spirit of God upon the spirit of man. There is a filtering down, a getting down into the very cells of the human soul and the impression on that soul by the Holy Ghost that this is true. That is what those disciples had never had before, and that is exactly what the Church does not have now. That is what we fundamentalist preachers wish we had and don't have, and that is why we are going so far astray to prove things. That, incidentally, is why this humble pulpit is never open to a man who wants to prove Christianity by means of appeal to external evidence. You can't do it to begin with, and I wouldn't do it to end with. We have something better.

Then, also, the Spirit gave a bright, emotional quality to their religion, and I grieve before my God over the lack of this in our day. The emotional quality isn't there. There is a sickliness about us all; we pump so hard trying to get a little drop of delight out of our old rusty well, and we write innumerable bouncy choruses, and we pump and pump until you can hear the old rusty thing squeak across forty acres. But it doesn't work.

Then He gave them direct spiritual authority. By that I mean He removed their fears, their questions, their apologies, and their doubts, and they had an authority that was founded upon life.

There is a great modern error which I want to mention: it is that the coming of the Spirit happened once for all, that the individual Christian is not affected by it. It is like the birth of Christ which happened once for all and the most excellent sermon on the birth of Christ would never have that birth repeated, and all the prayers in the wide world would never have Christ born again of the Virgin Mary. It is, they say, like the death and resurrection of Christ—never to be repeated. This error asserts that the coming of the Holy Spirit is an historic thing, an advance in the dispensational workings of God; but that it is all settled now and we need give no further thought to it. It is all here and we have it all, and if we believe in Christ that is it and there isn't anything more.

All right. Now everybody has a right to his or her view, if he thinks it is scriptural; but I would just like to ask some questions. I won't answer them; I'll just ask them, and you preach your own sermon.

Is the promise of the Father, with all its attendant riches of spiritual grace and power, intended to be for first-century Christians only? Does the new birth, which the first-century Christians had to have, suffice for all other Christians, or is the new birth which they had to have that which we have to have? Does the new birth have to be repeated in each Christian before it is valid, or did that first church get born again for us? Can you get born again by proxy? The fact that those first 120 were born again, does that mean that we don't have to be? Now you answer me.

You say, "No, certainly we agree that everybody has to have the new birth for himself, individually." All right, if that is true (and it is), is the fullness of the Spirit which those first Christians received enough? Does that work for you and me? They had the fullness; now they are dead. Does the fact that they were filled avail for me? You answer that question.

Again, I want to ask you, would a meal eaten by Saint Peter in the year 33 A. D. nourish me today? Would a good meal of barley cakes and milk, and honey spread on the barley cake— a good meal for a good Jew in Peter's day—nourish me today? No, Peter is dead, and I can't be nourished by what Peter ate.

Would the fullness of the Holy Ghost that Peter got in the upper chamber do for me today, or must I receive individually what Peter received?

What value would the fullness of the Spirit in the church in Jerusalem have for us today if it was done over there once for all and we can't have the same thing here? We are separated by 5,000 miles of water and by 1,900 years of time. Now what, that happened to them, can possibly avail for us?

I want to ask you some more questions: Do you see any similarity between the average one of us Christians buzzing around Chicago and those apostles? Are you ready to believe that we have just what they had, and that every believer in Chicago who accepts the Bible and is converted immediately enters into and now enjoys and possesses exactly what they did back there? Surely you know better than that!

This modern fundamentalism as we know it and of which we are a part—is it a satisfactory fulfillment of the expectations raised by the Father and Christ? Our Father who is in heaven raised certain high expectations of what He was going to do for His redeemed people. When His Son came to redeem those people, He heightened those expectations, raised them, clarified them, extended them, enlarged them, and emphasized them. He raised an expectation that was simply beyond words, too wonderful and beautiful and thrilling to imagine. I want to ask you: Is this level of Christianity which we fundamentalists in this city now enjoy what He meant by what He said?

Listen, brother. Our Lord Jesus Christ advertised that He was going away to the Father and He was going to send back for His people a wonderful gift, and He said, "Stay right here until it comes, because it will be the difference between failure and success to you."

Then the Spirit came. Was He equal to the advertising? Did they say, "Is this all He meant! Oh, it is disappointing!" No. The Scripture says they wondered. The word "wonder" is in their mouths and hearts. He gave so much more than He promised, because words were the promise and the Holy Ghost was the fulfillment.

The simple fact is that we believers are not up to what He gave us reason to expect. The only honest thing to do is admit this and do something about it. There certainly has been a vast breakdown somewhere between promise and fulfillment. That breakdown is not with our heavenly Father, for He always gives more than He promises.

Now I am going to ask that you reverently ponder this and set aside time and search the Scriptures, pray and yield, obey and believe, and see whether that which our Lord gave us reason to think could be the possession of the Church may not be ours in actual fulfillment and realization.

How to be Filled, with the Holy Spirit

Before we deal with the question of how to be filled with the Holy Spirit, there are some matters which first have to be settled. As believers you have to get them out of the way, and right here is where the difficulty arises. I have been afraid that my listeners might have gotten the idea somewhere that I had a how-to-be-filled-with-the-Spirit-in-five-easy-lessons doctrine, which I could give you. If you have any such vague ideas as that, I can only stand before you and say, "I am sorry"; because it isn't true; I can't give you such a course. There are some things, I say, that you have to get out of the way, settled. One of them is: Before you are filled with the Holy Spirit you must be sure that you can be filled.

Satan has opposed the doctrine of the Spirit-filled life about as bitterly as any other doctrine there is. He has confused it, opposed it, surrounded it with false notions and fears. He has blocked every effort of the Church of Christ to receive from the Father her divine and blood-bought patrimony. The Church has tragically neglected this great liberating truth—that there is now for the child of God a full and wonderful and completely satisfying anointing with the Holy Ghost.

So you have to be sure that it is for you. You must be sure that it is God's will for you; that is, that it is part of the total plan, that it is included and embraced within the work of Christ in redemption; that it is, as the old camp-meeting, praying folks used to say, "the purchase of His blood."

I might throw a bracket in here and say that whenever I use the neutral pronoun "it" I am talking about the gift. When I speak directly of the Holy Spirit, I shall use a personal pronoun, He or Him or His, referring to a person, for the Holy Spirit is not an it, but the gift of the Holy Spirit must necessarily in our English language be called "it."

You must, I say, be satisfied that this is nothing added or extra. The Spirit-filled life is not a special, deluxe edition of Christianity. It is part and parcel of the total plan of God for His people.

You must be satisfied that it is not abnormal. I admit that it is unusual, because there are so few people who walk in the light of it or enjoy it, but it is not abnormal. In a world where everybody was sick, health would be unusual, but it wouldn't be abnormal. This is unusual only because our spiritual lives are so wretchedly sick and so far down from where they should be.

You must be satisfied, again, that there is nothing about the Holy Spirit queer or strange or eerie. I believe it has been the work of the devil to surround the person of the Holy Spirit with an aura of queerness, or strangeness, so that the people of God feel that this Spirit-filled life is a life of being odd and peculiar, of being a bit uncanny.

That is not true, my friend! The devil manufactured that. He hatched it out, the same devil that once said to our ancient mother, "Yea, hath God said," and thus maligned God Almighty. That same devil has maligned the Holy Ghost. There is nothing eerie, nothing queer, nothing contrary to the normal operations of the human heart about the Holy Ghost. He is only the essence of Jesus imparted to believers. You read the four Gospels and see for yourself how wonderfully calm, pure, sane, simple, sweet, natural, and lovable Jesus was. Even philosophers who don't believe in His deity have to admit the lovableness of His character.

You must be sure of all this to the point of conviction. That is, you must be convinced to a point where you won't try to persuade God.

You don't have to persuade God at all. There is no persuasion necessary. Dr. Simpson used to say, "Being filled with the Spirit is as easy as breathing; you can simply breathe out and breathe in." He wrote a hymn to that effect. I am sorry that it is not a better hymn, because it is wonderful theology.

Unless you have arrived at this place in your listening and thinking and meditating and praying, where you know that the Spirit-filled life is for you, that there is no doubt about it—no book you read or sermon you heard, or tract somebody sent you is bothering you; you are restful about all this; you are convinced that in the blood of Jesus when He died on the cross there was included, as a purchase of that blood, your right to a full, Spirit-filled life—unless you are convinced of that, unless you are convinced that it isn't an added, unusual, extra, deluxe something that you have to go to God and beg and beat your fists on the chair to get, I recommend this to you: I recommend that you don't do anything about it yet except to meditate upon the Scriptures bearing on this truth. Go to the Word of God and to those parts of it which deal with the subject under discussion tonight and meditate upon them; for "faith cometh by hearing, and hearing by the word of God." Real faith springs not out of sermons but out of the Word of God and out of sermons only so far as they are of the Word of God. I recommend that you be calm and confident about this. Don't get excited, don't despond. The darkest hour is just before the dawn. It may be that this moment of discouragement which you are going through is preliminary to a sunburst of new and beautiful living, if you will follow on to know the Lord.

Remember, fear is of the flesh and panic is of the devil. Never fear and never get panicky. When they came to Jesus nobody except a hypocrite ever needed to fear Him. When a hypocrite came to Jesus He just sliced him to bits and sent him away bleeding from every pore. If they were ready to give up their sin and follow the Lord and they came in simplicity of heart and said, "Lord, what do You want me to do?" the Lord took all the time in the world to talk to them and explain to them and to correct any false impressions or wrong ideas they had. He is the sweetest, most understanding and wonderful Teacher in the world, and He never panics anybody. It is sin that does that. If there is a sense of panic upon your life, it may be because there is sin in that life of yours which you need to get rid of.

Again, before you can be filled with the Spirit you must desire to be filled. Here I meet with a certain amount of puzzlement. Somebody will say, "How is it that you say to us that we must desire to be filled, because you know we desire to be. Haven't we talked to you in person? Haven't we called you on the phone? Aren't we out here tonight to hear the sermon on the Holy Spirit? Isn't this all a comforting indication to you that we are desirous of being filled with the Holy Spirit?"

Not necessarily, and I will explain why. For instance, are you sure that you want to be possessed by a spirit other than your own? Even though that spirit be the pure Spirit of God? even though He be the very gentle essence of the gentle Jesus? even though He be sane and pure and free? even though He be wisdom personified, wisdom Himself, even though He have a healing, precious ointment to distill? even though He be loving as the heart of God? That Spirit, if He ever possesses you, will be the Lord of your Life!

I ask you, Do you want Him to be Lord of your life? That you want His benefits, I know. I take that for granted. But do you want to be possessed by Him? Do you want to hand the keys of your soul over to the Holy Spirit and say, "Lord, from now on I don't even have a key to my own house. I come and go as Thou tellest me"? Are you willing to give the office of your business establishment, your soul, over to the Lord and say to Jesus,

"You sit in this chair and handle these telephones and boss the staff and be Lord of this outfit"? That is what I mean. Are you sure you want this? Are you sure that you desire it?

Are you sure that you want your personality to be taken over by One who will expect obedience to the written and living Word? Are you sure that you want your personality to be taken over by One who will not tolerate the self sins? For instance, self-love. You can no more have the Holy Ghost and have self-love than you can have purity and impurity at the same moment in the same place. He will not permit you to indulge self-confidence. Self-love, self-confidence, self-righteousness, self-admiration, self-aggrandizement, and self-pity are under the interdiction of God Almighty, and He cannot send His mighty Spirit to possess the heart where these things are.

Again, I ask you if you desire to have your personality taken over by One who stands in sharp opposition to the world's easy ways? No tolerance of evil, no smiling at crooked jokes, no laughing off things that God hates. The Spirit of God, if He takes over, will bring you into opposition to the world just as Jesus was brought into opposition to it. The world crucified Jesus because they couldn't stand Him! There was something in Him that rebuked them and they hated Him for it and finally crucified Him. The world hates the Holy Ghost as bad as they ever hated Jesus, the One from whom He proceeds. Are you sure, brother? You want His help, yes; you want a lot of His benefits, yes; but are you willing to go with Him in His opposition to the easygoing ways of the world? If you are not, you needn't apply for anything more than you have, because you don't want Him; you only think you do!

Again, are you sure that you need to be filled? Can't you get along the way you are? You have been doing fairly well: You pray, you read your Bible, you give to missions, you enjoy singing hymns, you thank God you don't drink or gamble or attend theaters, that you are honest, that you have prayer at home. You are glad about all this. Can't you get along like that? Are you sure you need any more than that? I want to be fair with you. I want to do what Jesus did: He turned around to them when they were following Him and told them the truth. I don't want to take you in under false pretense. "Are you sure you want to follow Me?" He asked, and a great many turned away. But Peter said, "Lord, to whom shall we go? thou hast the words of eternal life." And the crowd that wouldn't turn away was the crowd that made history. The crowd that wouldn't turn back was the crowd that was there when the Holy Ghost came and filled all the place where they were sitting. The crowd that turned back never knew what it was all about.

But maybe you feel in your heart that you just can't go on as you are, that the level of spirituality to which you know yourself called is way beyond you. If you feel that there is something that you must have or your heart will never be satisfied, that there are levels of spirituality, mystic deeps and heights of spiritual communion, purity and power that you have never known, that there is fruit which you know you should bear and do not, victory which you know you should have and have not—I would say, "(Come on," because God has something for you tonight.

There is a spiritual loneliness, an inner aloneness, an inner place where God brings the seeker, where he is as lonely as if there were not another member of the Church anywhere in the world. Ah, when you come there, there is a darkness of mind, an emptiness of heart, a loneliness of soul, but it is preliminary to the daybreak. O God, bring us, somehow, to the daybreak!

Here is how to receive. First, present your body to Him (Rom. 12: 1, 2). God can't fill what He can't have. Now I ask you: Are you ready to present your body with all of its functions and all that it contains—your mind, your personality, your spirit, your love, your ambitions, your all? That is the first thing. That is a simple, easy act—presenting the body. Are you willing to do it?

Now the second thing is to ask (Luke 11: 9-11), and I set aside all theological objections to this text. They say that is not for today. Well, why did the Lord leave it in the Bible then? Why didn't He put it somewhere else; why did He put it where I could see it if He didn't want me to believe it? It is all for us, and if the Lord wanted to do it, He could give it without our asking, but He chooses to have us ask. "Ask of me, and I will give thee" is always God's order; so why not ask?

Acts 5: 32 tells us the third thing to do. God gives His Holy Spirit to them that obey Him. Are you ready to obey and do what you are asked to do? What would that be? Simply to live by the Scriptures as you understand them. Simple, but revolutionary.

The next thing is, have faith (Gal. 3: 2). We receive Him by faith as we receive the Lord in salvation by faith. He comes as a gift of God to us in power. First He comes in some degree and measure when we are converted, otherwise we couldn't be converted. Without Him we couldn't be born again, because we are born of the Spirit. But I am talking about something different now, an advance over that. I am talking about His coming and possessing the full body and mind and life and heart, taking the whole personality over, gently, but directly and bluntly, and making it His, so that we may become a habitation of God through the Spirit.

So now suppose we sing. Let us sing The Comforter Has Come, because He has come. If He hasn't come to your heart in fullness, He will; but He has come to the earth. He is here and ready, when we present our vessel, to fill our vessel if we will ask and believe. Will you do it?

HOW TO CULTIVATE THE SPIRIT'S COMPANIONSHIP

"Can two walk together, except they be agreed?"
Amos 3: 3.

Now This is what is known as a rhetorical question; it is equivalent to a positive declaration that two cannot walk together except they be agreed, and for two to walk together they must be in some sense one.

They also have to agree that they want tc walk together, and they have to agree that it is to their advantage to travel together. I think you will see that it all adds up to this: For two to walk together voluntarily they must be, in some sense, one.

I am talking now about how we can cultivate the Spirit's fellowship, how we can walk with Him day by day and hour by hour—and you won't object if I say "you." Sometimes we preachers preach in the third person, and you can develop a habit of thinking in the third person. We don't talk about "us"; we talk about "they." I don't like that. I think we ought to get personal about this.

There are some of you who are not ready for this sermon at all. You are trying to face both ways at once. You are trying to take some of this world and to get some of that world over yonder. You are a Christian, but I am talking about an advance upon the first early stages of salvation and the cultivation of the presence of the Holy Ghost, so that He may illuminate and bless and lift and purify and direct your life. You are not ready for this, because you haven't given up all that you might have the All. You want some, but you don't want all; that is the reason you are not ready.

You who have not given up the world will not be able to understand what I am talking about. You want Christianity for its insurance value. You want just what a man wants when he takes out a policy on his life, or his car, or his house. You don't want modernism, because it hasn't any insurance value. You are willing to support this proposition financially. He would be a poor man who would want insurance and not be willing to pay for it. If Jesus Christ died for you on the cross you are very happy about that because it means you won't be brought into judgment, but have passed from death into life. You are willing to live reasonably well, because that is the premium you are paying for the guarantee that God will bless you while you live and take you home to heaven when you die!

You may not be ready because your conception of religion is social and not spiritual. There are people like that. They have watered down the religion of the New Testament until it has no strength in it. They have introduced the water of their own opinion into it, until it has no taste left. They are socially minded. This is as far as it goes with them. People like that may be saved. I am not prepared to say that they are not saved, but I am prepared to say that they are not ready for what I am talking about. The gospel of Christ is essentially spiritual, and Christian truth working upon human souls by the Holy Ghost makes Christian men and women spiritual.

I don't like to say this, but I think that some of you may not be ready for this message because you are more influenced by the world than you are by the New Testament. I am perfectly certain that I could rake up fifteen boxcar loads of fundamentalist Christians this hour in the city of Chicago who are more influenced in their whole outlook by Hollywood than they are by the Lord Jesus Christ. I am positive that much that passes for the gospel in our day is very little more than a very mild case of orthodox religion grafted on to a heart that is sold out to the world in its pleasures and tastes and ambitions.

The kind of teaching that I have been giving has disturbed some people. I am not going to apologize at all, because, necessarily, if I have been traveling along thinking I am all right and there comes a man of God and tells me that there is yet much land to be possessed, it will disturb me. That is the preliminary twinge that comes to the soul that wants to know God. Whenever the Word of God hits us, it disturbs us. So don't be disturbed by the disturbance. Remember that it is quite normal. God has to jar us loose.

But there are some who are prepared. They are those who have made the grand, sweet committal. They have seen heaven draw nearer and earth recede; the things of this world have become less and less attractive, and the things of heaven have begun to pull and pull as the moon pulls at the sea, and they are prepared now. So I am going to give you these few little pointers to help you into a better life.

Point one is that the Holy Spirit is a living person. He is the third Person of the Trinity. He is Himself God, and as a Person, He can be cultivated; He can be wooed and cultivated the same as any person can be. People grow on us, and the Holy Spirit, being a Person, can grow on us.

The second point is: Be engrossed with Jesus Christ. Honor Him. John said: "But this spake he of the Spirit, which they that believe on him should receive: for the Holy Ghost was not yet given; because that Jesus was not yet glorified."

I ask you to note that the Spirit was given when Jesus was glorified. Now that is a principle. Remember that He came and spread Himself out as a flood upon the people because Jesus was glorified. He established a principle, and He will never, never flood the life of any man except the man in whom Jesus is glorified. Therefore, if you dedicate yourself to the glory of Jesus, the Holy Ghost will become the aggressor and will seek to know you and raise you and illumine you and fill you and bless you. Honoring Jesus Christ is doing the things which Jesus told you to do, trusting Him as your All, following Him as your Shepherd, and obeying Him fully.

Let's cultivate the Holy Ghost by honoring the Lord Jesus. As we honor Jesus, the Spirit of God becomes glad within us. He ceases to hold back, He relaxes and becomes intimate and communes and imparts Himself; and the sun comes up and heaven comes near as Jesus Christ becomes our all in all.

To glorify Jesus is the business of the Church, and to glorify Jesus is the work of the Holy Ghost. I can walk with Him when I am doing the same things He is doing, and go the same way He is going and travel at the same speed He is traveling. I must be engrossed with Jesus Christ. I must honor Him. "If any man serve me, him will my Father honour" (John 12: 26). So let's honor the Lord Jesus. Not only theologically, but let's honor Him personally.

The third point is: Let's walk in righteousness. The grace of God that bringeth salvation also teaches the heart that we should deny ungodliness and worldly lusts and live soberly and righteously and godly in this present world. There you have the three dimensions of life. Soberly—that is me. Righteously— that is my fellowman. Godly—that is God. Let us not make the mistake of thinking we can be spiritual and not be good. Let's not make the mistake of thinking we can walk with the Holy Ghost and go a wrong or a dirty or an unrighteous way, for how can two walk together except they be agreed? He is the Holy Spirit, and if I walk an unholy way, how can I fellowship with Him?

The fourth is: Make your thoughts a clean sanctuary. To God, our thoughts are things. Our thoughts are the decorations inside the sanctuary where we live. If our thoughts are purified by the blood of Christ, we are living in a clean room no matter if we are wearing overalls covered with grease. Your thoughts pretty much decide the mood and weather and climate inside your heart, and God considers your thoughts as part of you. Thoughts of peace, thoughts of pity, thoughts of mercy, thoughts of kindness, thoughts of charity, thoughts of God, thoughts of the Son of God-these are pure things, good things, and high things. Therefore, if you would cultivate the Spirit's acquaintance, you must get hold of your thoughts and not allow your mind to be a wilderness in which every kind of unclean beast roams and bird flies. You must have a clean heart.

Point five: Let us seek to know Him in the Word. It is in the Word we will find the Holy Spirit. Don't read too many other things. Some of you will say, "Look who's talking!" Well, go ahead and say it, I don't mind; but I am reading fewer and fewer things as I get older, not because I am losing interest in this great, big, old suffering world, but because I am gaining interest in that other world above. So I say, don't try to know everything. You can't. Find Him in the Word, for the Holy Ghost wrote this Book. He inspired it, and He will be revealed in its pages.

What is the word when we come to the Bible? It is meditate. We are to come to the Bible and meditate. That is what the old saints did. They meditated. They laid the Bible on the old-fashioned handmade chair, got down on the old, scrubbed board floor and meditated on the Word. As they meditated, faith mounted. The Spirit and faith illuminated. They had nothing but a Bible with fine print and narrow margins and poor paper, but they knew their Bible better than some of us with all of our helps. Let's practice the art of Bible meditation.

Now please don't grab that phrase and go out and form a club. Don't do it! Just meditate. That is what we need. We are organized to death already. Let's just be plain Christians. Let's open our Bible, spread it out on the chair, and meditate on it. It will open itself to us, and the Spirit of God will come and brood over it.

So be a Bible meditator. I challenge you: Try it for a month and see how it works. Put away questions and answers and the filling in of blank lines about Noah. Put all that cheap trash away and take a Bible, open it, get on your knees and say, "Father, here I am. Begin to teach me." He will begin to teach you, and He will teach you about Himself and about Jesus and about God and about the Word and about life and death and heaven and hell, and about His own Presence.

I have just one more point: Cultivate the art of recognizing the presence of the Spirit everywhere. Get acquainted with the Holy Ghost and then begin to cultivate His presence. When you wake in the morning, in place of burying your head behind the Tribune, couldn't you get in just a few thoughts of God while you eat your grapefruit?

Remember, cultivating the Holy Ghost's acquaintance is a job. It is something you do, and yet it is so easy and delightful. It is like cultivating your baby's acquaintance. You know when you first look at the little wrinkled fellow, yelling, all mouth, you don't know him. He is a little stranger to you. Then you begin to cultivate him, and he smiles. (It isn't a smile at all. He has colic! You think it is a smile, and it is such a delight.) Pretty soon he wiggles an arm, and you think he is waving at you. Then he gurgles and you think he said "Mama." You get acquainted!

Is this for ministers? This is for ministers, certainly. Is it for housewives? Yes, housewives, and clerks and milkmen and students. If you will thus see it and thus believe it and thus surrender to it, there won't be a secular stone in the pavement. There won't be a common, profane deed that you will ever do. The most menial task can become a priestly ministration when the Holy Ghost takes over and Christ becomes your all in all.

www.ingramcontent.com/pod-product-compliance
Lightning Source LLC
Chambersburg PA
CBHW020549080526
44583CB00013B/1062